Active Appreciation: How to Develop Employees Who Exceed Expectations

Paula Schwartz

ISBN: 1500907340
ISBN 13: 9781500907341

For Mom and Dicky
with sincere appreciation

Conversations build a culture. Culture builds a company. There are few conversations more powerful in building a strong, engaging, progressive culture than the conversations of *active appreciation*. These conversations speak of the past, present, and future.

They recognize what someone has done in the past. They acknowledge your understanding of the commitment and character those acts required and instill a sense of pride and accomplishment in the present. And they convey your gratitude for the impact those acts will have in the future.

If you want to truly shape the culture of your business and actively engage your team in the future, practice and embrace active appreciation.

Contents

Introduction

Iremember, as a young wife, hearing the words, "Love isn't something you *have*, it's something you *do*." The intent of this book is to convince you that the same is true of appreciation.

A few weeks ago, I shared the phrase below that a friend had posted on Facebook:

A Person Who Feels Appreciated Will Exceed Expectations

I shared it because it resonated with me. It was one of those commonsense ideas that I wished some of my bosses had known. Apparently it resonated with other colleagues and friends as well, because within three days, a significant group of my colleagues, contacts, and peers had shared the photo or made a comment about it. To me, that was a clear signal. There is a loud and resounding ring of truth in these words.

As I looked at my own personal career and the different consulting projects I have worked on, I can vividly recall the times I felt appreciated, and, with just as much emotion (if not more), I can also recall the times when I did not. The shocking realization was that the times I felt unappreciated severely outweighed the times I felt acknowledged and appreciated.

Almost without exception, I work with highly skilled, motivated, intelligent consultants and clients who are committed to business performance. They have even gone so far as to center their company's vision and priorities around valuing people. And yet so many of my colleagues do not feel appreciated on an *individual* basis for what they contribute. The other ironic piece of this puzzle is that we—this group of overwhelmed, unmotivated colleagues and I who do not feel appreciated—have been working on consulting projects *with the intention of creating or improving employee engagement!*

Richard Lukesh, owner of the website Your Part Time HR Manager, cites his favorite question to ask clients about problem employees: "Were they dead when you hired them, or did you kill them?" (See http://www.yourparttimehrmanager.com.)

Any experienced manager can relate to the experience of disengaged employees who show up and just go through each day, dragging through the motions of the minimum requirements of their jobs, looking more like zombies than members of a team. The sad probability is that, with few exceptions, when those employees were first hired, they were genuinely excited and saw great opportunities ahead for the company and for themselves. At some point, those visions became fantasies, and they stopped believing that their "dream job" would ever be more than a paycheck.

If I were to ask the consultants and clients I have worked with, "Do you appreciate the people who work for you?" they would emphatically say, "Yes!" And I have no doubt that is true for them. They feel an appreciation for me and for all (well, OK, *most*) of the people who work for them. But, at the end of the day, appreciation must go further than a perception or feeling that employers, supervisors, or colleagues have for the people they work with. It must be translated into actions that resonate with employees, that give them the sense that they are valued for their individual contribution, and that convince them that their efforts are making a difference. This is what I call *active appreciation.*

At the end of the day, we all just want to know that what we do matters. Here's how you do that...

One

Appreciation Does Not Just Happen

Appreciation Does Not Just Happen

A great deal of research has been done on why employees leave. Survey after survey, list after list, they all strike a similar chord: *I do not like my relationship with my boss. I am not making a contribution. I have no say in my job or career path. I never hear anything positive. My team does not support me. I do not get recognized for what I do.* The list goes on, but it all boils down to one simple fact: people leave because they do not feel that their opinion, their work, or their accomplishments are appreciated. This tells us that active appreciation is uncommon.

Before we get too far into exploring this assumption, let's define appreciation. The *Merriam-Webster Dictionary* defines appreciation as follows:

(1) a feeling of being grateful for something; (2) an ability to understand the worth, quality, or importance of something, an ability to appreciate something; and (3) full awareness or understanding of something.

We want to take this definition further, to encompass the actions that transfer or communicate that feeling, understanding, and awareness to the employees' feeling of appreciation.

As I stated in the introduction, to move employees from the disillusionment, resignation, and apathy that is creeping toward them, appreciation cannot just be something you *have*; rather, it must become something you *do*. To move employees toward loyalty, engagement, and personal investment in your team's success, your appreciation must become *active*.

When I first researched the term *active appreciation*, I was hoping I had come up with something original. But it's already a real term used in accounting. Its definition is "an increase in the value of an asset as a result of its owner's action." What a great way of looking at my use of the phrase!

When we consider our human capital as our most valuable asset, active appreciation allows for that increase in value by helping employees who exceed expectations engage in our business success and find true satisfaction in their job.

I remember attending a conference in Spain on human capital where a speaker discussed the intangible assets section of a balance sheet. While brand reputation and goodwill are often included in the value of a company, the speaker pointed out that we rarely recognize the decrease in value a company experiences, especially on its balance sheet, when skilled labor, innovation, business relationships, and *knowledge capital* walk out the door through attrition.

A worldwide study by Towers Watson found that "[t]he single highest driver of engagement is whether or not workers feel their managers are genuinely interested in their well-being."[1]

Several of my clients are large, global organizations that define company values and visions with words like *caring, people focused,* and *valuing employees,* and yet in almost every industry, we find that some of the most common business challenges being faced today are employee retention, employee engagement, and job satisfaction.

---

[1] See http://www.towerswatson.com/assets/pdf/2012-Towers-Watson-Global-Workforce-Study.pdf.

Leaders do not have the leisure of pointing the finger and saying, "It's not me; it's them." There is no value in suggesting that I, as a leader, feel appreciation for people and that whether or not they experience it is not my problem but theirs. My people's obstacles to performance and job satisfaction are mine. And their lack of feeling appreciated is a true obstacle. It is the leader's role to motivate people to do their jobs well and to want to keep doing so. All of the warm feelings in the world, if not communicated, do not make a difference for the individuals doing the work.

One example that hits close to home is my mother. She has worked in the office next to my husband as his bookkeeper and office manager for twenty-one years. She has a very strong work ethic; after she retired, three people had to be hired to cover for the various tasks she had performed. I lived with her boss, and I knew how much he valued and appreciated her. He gave her bonuses and raises and checked in on her frequently to see how things were going. He knew he could always count on her to meet deadlines and have everything work out, and he constantly tried to thank her. And yet, upon her retirement, she finally shared with me how unappreciated she had always felt by him and his partners. There was a definite disconnect between the appreciation he and his partners felt for her and the appreciation she experienced. We will look more at how this could have been resolved in a later chapter, "Acts of Appreciation." But the point to take away is that his feelings of appreciation, while sincere, were not effective in encouraging her engagement.

Another example is a friend who is a rig manager on a drillship for an offshore drilling contractor and one of the most diligent and well-intended young managers I have encountered. He works in a very dynamic environment with particular challenges tied to regulatory requirements and the varying cultures of the local labor he manages. I received a text from him one day that simply stated, "Sometimes, I struggle to stay positive."

So many of the surveys done on job satisfaction and why employees leave have quotes about how they only hear from their managers when there is a problem or that they only receive negative feedback. The pressures and emotions associated with breakdowns and poor performance can render a heavy burden to a conscientious, well-intended frontline manager. How do you actively express appreciation during these challenges?

My friend was in the thick of a negative situation and feeling the pressure. I give him credit for being the type of employee who recognizes when things are getting negative and reaches out to colleagues or managers for positive encouragement. But be aware: this practice is rare. All too often employees sink deeper into the negative and never come out, blaming a lack of support or appreciation from their peers and supervisors.

Consider what happens to an asset in the absence of active appreciation. It falls into decline. Its performance decreases. I love my house. I love the flowers in the yard and the natural light that the large, uncurtained windows allow. I love the hardwood floors and the big room in the front where my piano fits so perfectly. But if I do not maintain it, it will decline. I must, on occasion, condition the hardwood floors, maintain the garden, and clean the windows. If I neglect these things, the house's value will decrease. Almost always, the decline is gradual. Many of us do not even recognize some of the signs that the conditions of our home are declining until we're preparing to sell it and our real estate agent makes that funny face when she walks around, assessing it. Or, worse yet, when our mother-in-law comes to visit.

Similarly, for all of the good intentions, awareness, and understanding by business leaders of the critical value and contributions employees provide to the success of their organization, their people are not encouraged, developed, or acknowledged enough to avoid the decline. Active appreciation is a vital element in the upkeep of motivated employees.

Two

What Gets in the Way?

What Gets in the Way?

So what are we doing wrong? How is it that managers and entire organizations who strategize to be people focused and value their employees are missing the mark on active appreciation? The common mistakes discussed below will help illuminate opportunities to shift how we interact with one another to create that culture of active appreciation. The bottom line is that actions speak louder than words.

Let's discuss four common mistakes well-intended people make:

1. Squeaky wheel syndrome
2. Isn't paying them enough?

3. The generic thank-you is not apprecia-
    tion.
4. Recognition versus appreciation

Squeaky Wheel Syndrome

By nature, we are problem solvers. Thus, problems get a lot of our attention. People who have had to prove themselves up through the ranks to management have seen how much more attention gets paid to the employee who doesn't quite finish the job or manage the details. This leaves the ones who do perform well working on their own, with little interaction with management. All too often, their diligence and reliability is rewarded with an occasional pat on the back and the "privilege" of getting their own work done while also carrying the load for the poor performers.

In a salary discussion, Dave, a new supervisor, told his employer, "Listen, it doesn't matter what you pay me; you are going to get a high quality of work because I have a work ethic that simply doesn't allow for anything else." That might not have been his smartest move in a salary negotiation! They agreed to start him at the same salary as his peers and allow him the chance to prove himself. He did so, and received a raise the next year. But so did his peers—even the ones who were not pulling their weight! Granted, he made a little more, but the fact that problem employees were still getting the standard increase made him a bit hot under the collar.

His manager was smart and knew that he was creative and enjoyed working on his own to create new, outside-the-box solutions. She believed the best way to incentivize him was to allow him to work on his own. She was right, and he did enjoy the freedom of creating new solutions. However, when he needed time with her to discuss or promote his ideas, she was often busy and overwhelmed with her problem workers. She told him to go ahead and do what needed to be done and gave him the freedom to run with his ideas. But, without management commitment or involvement in his projects, he often butted heads with the other departments he needed to work with in order to implement his solutions. He eventually felt defeated and unable to make the contributions he so wanted to, and he left.

This manager is certainly not alone in her approach. The lesson she quickly learned was that focusing on what needed to be fixed by giving more time to the problem workers rarely improved their performance. The poor performers felt unsuccessful. The company fell into a cycle of good performers working hard on their own to sustain the business and poor performers having their roles changed, minimized, and micromanaged to the point that they were ineffective.

Within a short period of time, the company saw its high performers beginning to leave. Some moved on to work with competitors. Others went to work for their current clients. Eventually, the majority of people who remained with the company were the poor performers who had nowhere else to go. It became nearly impossible for the manager to deliver the team results she was committed to.

A powerful lesson comes from Susan Scott's book *Fierce Conversations*: "Burnout doesn't occur because we're solving problems; it occurs because we've been trying to solve the same problem over and over."

I know this manager and have no doubt that she appreciated the efforts and contributions of all of her employees, *especially* her top performers who worked so well independently. She read books, asked for advice, and worked very hard to create a positive work environment for everyone. But, despite her efforts, no one really felt appreciated. Focusing on the problems simply got in the way.

Isn't Paying Them Enough?

This is a common belief among managers: My people are here to do a job. They are paid for that work. That should be enough.

In a perfect world, that might be true. But the numerous surveys, research studies, and reports all say the same thing...paying them simply isn't enough.

For one thing, they can go anywhere and get paid. Many industries are struggling to retain skilled labor. When competitors are constantly offering the same pay (or sometimes more) for the same work, with the promise of a more attractive work environment, we must do more to make our strong performers want to stay.

Even bonuses do not accomplish active appreciation. Many companies have gotten to the point where bonuses are expected for average performance. The only people who do not get bonuses are the people who do not meet their goals. Otherwise, if our team members show up every day and just do their jobs, they expect that bonus. This minimizes the bonus as an effective way to communicate active appreciation, especially for your top performers.

Some people do feel appreciated when they receive an unexpected or higher-than-expected raise. (We will talk more about individual preferences for feeling appreciation in a later chapter.) But more money does not always translate into more engagement. In the vast data available on why people leave jobs, money is rarely the most important factor. The most commonly cited factor in why people leave is their relationship with their boss or supervisor. Active appreciation plays a large part in that relationship.

The Generic Thank-You Is Not Appreciation

This is where the phrase *actions speak louder than words* gets used the most. So many times, managers are unsure how to express active appreciation because, no matter what they say, their employees have longstanding, immovable beliefs about what their managers think. Saying thank you is not going to change that. How does your thank-you line up with your actions?

Let's say you work with a colleague, Bob, who has been working on a project for years. Bob has built this project from the ground up, and, through the process, has mentored and trained several other team members in his particular project and even developed a manual for them. The project has been successful, and your company has decided to expand its offering of this product or service. Your management team wants someone with industry credentials to head up the new, expanded project team. They find someone and hire him. When the new project manager calls his first meeting with the project team, he points out that Bob has been there since day one and probably knows more about the specifics of the project than him. During the meeting, Bob answers many of the questions and refers to his manual several times. At the end of the meeting, you hear a member of the management team casually say, "Thanks for your input, Bob!" and then usher the new project manager into a room to discuss strategy and plans to move forward.

Do you think Bob felt appreciated? How did his manager demonstrate appreciation?

Another example is the common practice of thanking everyone for taking the time to attend a meeting or training session. It is important that we take the time to use active appreciation with people who are coming in on their time off or sacrificing work that needs to be done to attend a meeting or training. Otherwise, their thoughts about the sacrifices and efforts required to be there could distract them and create an obstacle to accomplishing the purpose of the meeting or training. If their sacrifices and efforts are addressed in a generic way to the group, without acknowledging the individual efforts and without clearly communicating the value and impact their participation will provide, the thank-you will fall on deaf ears. It becomes something you say that is met with an eye roll and a look at the watch.

Also, the generic thank-you will not likely carry the weight of a personal expression of gratitude. Similar to the annual raise where "everybody gets one," if the star performer gets the same thank-you as the poor performer, they will both be left wondering if anyone has really noticed what they have done.

In order for a thank-you to communicate active appreciation, it cannot be generic. It must be delivered in a way that is personal and applicable to the person receiving it, and it must be specific about what the person provided. I will say more about how to use thank-you's as active appreciation in the next chapter.

Recognition versus Appreciation

Recognition tends to be given based on outcomes achieved by individuals or teams. Active appreciation should recognize the value of what someone did or contributed personally, regardless of the outcome. To communicate appreciation, we must dig deeper to recognize what individuals contribute to the effort.

The area of safety is a prime opportunity to distinguish between recognition and active appreciation. You can recognize someone for going 365 days without a workplace injury or incident. This often comes in the form of plaques or awards of varying types. But in order to foster and build a culture where safety is consistent, you want to use active appreciation as positive reinforcement to the people who took the extra time to do the job right or who had the courage to speak up when someone was at risk. Identifying and rewarding the actions that contribute to the desired culture will build and sustain that culture.

While public recognition is often valued, not everyone likes being singled out in public. It is important to know your people and what they prefer.

Another approach that is commonly cited as expressed appreciation is what managers call the sandwich approach. They sandwich the issue between recognition of things someone is doing well. For example, I have heard someone start a meeting with, "The team is producing some good results, and we got some good feedback on your safety record, but we need to talk about the constant equipment failures we've been having." This does not communicate appreciation or recognition. It might ease you into the conversation you really want to have, which is addressing the equipment failures, but if you truly want the team to be acknowledged and feel appreciation for their safety record or good results, you must find a way to do so without ending the conversation with a problem.

So we are getting clearer about what active appreciation is *not*. In order to avoid the squeaky wheel syndrome of focusing only on the problem, we should spend some time exploring how we can effectively transfer those feelings of appreciation so that our employees are motivated to continue performing well.

Three

Acts of Appreciation

Acts of Appreciation

In his book *7 Habits of Highly Effective People,* Steven Covey wrote, "Next to physical survival, the greatest need of a human being is psychological survival, to be understood, to be affirmed, to be validated, to be appreciated."

As discussed in the previous chapter, appreciation must be more than a feeling. You cannot simply let your appreciation live in your mind and assume it is felt by the people you appreciate. Your appreciation must take the form of actions that allow those you appreciate to feel understood, acknowledged, valued, and proud of their work.

As much as I wish I had the formula for making anyone feel appreciated at any time, such a formula cannot exist. If we were dealing with something like hitting a golf ball or building a fence, I could give you step-by-step instructions that could be practiced and perfected in such a way that they would yield a similar result every time. Unfortunately, we are not dealing with a ball and a stick or a hammer and wood. We are dealing with human beings. In my experience, if you hit five different golf balls with the same club, the same way, the results would be similar. However, if you were to communicate with five different human beings in exactly the same way, you would experience five very different responses. Everyone is different! In order to make the impact you want, you must tailor each approach to the individual preferences and experiences of the people you are working with.

The first step in being effective at showing appreciation is knowing who you are talking to. This is well stated by Marcus Buckingham and Donald Clifton in their book *Now, Discover Your Strengths*, where they tell us, "To excel as a manager, to turn your people's talents into productive, powerful strengths, requires an additional all-important ingredient. Lacking this ingredient, [...] you will never reach excellence. The all-important ingredient is individualization."

There are many ways to find out your employees' preferences for acknowledgment and appreciation. Much of it lies in their personalities. Some may prefer public acknowledgment, others prefer financial reward, while some others (like my mom in the example earlier) would just like to have someone step in and help carry some of the load. We will discuss more about learning your employees' preferences in the next chapter.

Below you will find a short list of acts of appreciation. While the list is by no means exhaustive, it provides a launching point from which you can begin to take action and demonstrate you care through active appreciation.

1. Ask for feedback and advice.
2. Offer support.
3. Thank them personally.
4. Recognize them in public.
5. Acknowledge them.
6. Reciprocate.

Ask for Feedback and Advice

It's nice to tell people that you appreciate their work and expertise, but getting their input on what they do to be successful and what challenges they face will give them the sense that you truly value what they think and do.

Managers who allow their team to contribute to the improvement of their processes develop strong teams. This allows the employees to feel like they are contributing to more than just production or customer service. Providing their own personal perspective, ideas, and ingenuity toward the success of the team and the organization creates a feeling of contribution that is quickly translated into that rare commodity: employee ownership.

Telling people you value their ideas and approach to their work is just words. Active appreciation requires that you take actions that engage them and their individual contributions toward the success and future of their team. Actions speak louder than words: *ask for their input.*

Offer Support

Often the people we respect the most are the ones who seem to get so much done. When we need to add something to their already-full workload, they never blink an eye; they take it on, and invariably they get it all done. (This was the case with my mother at my husband's office.) Sometimes the best way to truly let your employees know you appreciate them is to roll up your sleeves and work with them to get things done. If they work late every night, choose a night and stay late with them. This active appreciation will let them know you are not taking advantage of their strong work ethic.

One challenge with this type of worker is that they will never raise the white flag; even if you ask if they need help, they will decline and find a way to get it all done, alone. Don't ask. Just show up and take something off their plate. Then, when you say that you appreciate all that they do, they can believe that you have a sense of what that is and the challenges they face...because you have done it with them! *And* you can be specific when you acknowledge how well they deal with the challenges and workload.

Telling someone thank you for getting so much done is nice, but it does not engender the feelings of pride and acknowledgment that enlist engagement. You must take actions that demonstrate your commitment to helping this valuable asset get the job done. Actions speak louder than words—*pitch in!*

Thank Them Personally

This is different from the generic thank-you I described in the previous chapter. A personal thank-you involves a one-on-one conversation that acknowledges the personal attributes or character traits the person possesses that contribute to the performance of the team.

Returning to the example of Bob and the project manager in the last chapter, the member of the management team could have gone to Bob after the meeting and said, "You really know your stuff. Thank you for stepping in and sharing what you know. It takes generosity to do that with someone new coming in, and it didn't go unnoticed. I appreciate your contribution." That would have created a completely different experience for Bob. Granted, they are still *just words*. That makes the thank-you less effective, but it is a start. The next step is taking actions to encourage and maximize Bob's involvement in the project.

Who do you appreciate? Take a moment to consider *why* you appreciate them. What do they provide? What is special about them that allows you to count on them for specific things?

Now ask yourself how you can communicate that specific appreciation. Doing so will make them feel known and proud of their unique contributions. Jon Katzenbach wrote a whole book on *Why Pride Matters More Than Money*. Employees who take pride in their work and accomplishments are less likely to leave and more willing to take on the team's responsibilities as their own.

Saying thank you is polite and sounds nice. But the employees you lead are looking for the actions that demonstrate what you are saying. Make your thank-yous personal, demonstrating your understanding of what people contribute. And then take actions to encourage and utilize those contributions. Actions speak louder than words—with your thank-yous, *follow up with action.*

Recognize Them in Public

Unlike the standard award presentation, public appreciation identifies a team member's personal contribution to the team. You can recognize someone for being with the company for twenty years, but to instill that appreciation so that they feel it, get personal about what they have provided by working in different roles throughout their tenure, the challenges they have faced, and the difference they have made.

Another method of public appreciation is sharing your own successes. When you are praised or recognized for your team's achievements, take the opportunity to share with your boss, with your peers, or anyone who will listen, the individual contributions of the people on your team that made your success possible. This goes beyond the casual, "I could not have done it without my team." Identify individual contributions and brag on them. Few things call people to bring forth more effort and energy from people than hearing someone brag about them.

For example, by introducing a new maintenance supervisor to your boss as "the new guy who is really bringing everyone up to a new level on meeting our maintenance deadlines," you have given him pride in the work he has done thus far and a standard for the work he will do in the future. Pride is an emotional response. These internal, emotional drivers can call average workers to rise to the level you speak of. That new maintenance supervisor has now been given a higher standard to work from because of who you say he is.

A public announcement about results and outcomes is a good start. To instill pride, make the public recognition personal, reminding your team and that individual of the unique qualities he or she brings and the difference those qualities make to your success. Actions speak louder than words—*make it personal!*

Acknowledge Them

Acknowledgment is part of active appreciation. It involves acknowledging contributions, even if they're obvious, and appreciating them. For example, at the end of some of the trainings I have led for men who work on offshore rigs, I take some time to acknowledge them for what they do. I remind them that they are responsible for billions of dollars of equipment, hundreds of lives, and their company's relationship with its customers and employees. Now, this is not news. They know this. They live it every day. It is their job. It is what they do. But taking a moment to acknowledge the responsibility they take on every day gives them a sense of appreciation for the challenges they face and the efforts they put into managing them.

You can acknowledge someone for working through a power outage, for working on the week of her daughter's wedding, for being brilliant at creating pivot tables, or for taking a million other actions that are known but rarely spoken of. Taking the time to do so creates a sense of team and provides active appreciation.

Acknowledgment might seem unnecessary in that you are stating something that everyone already knows; however, taking the time to remind your team of the efforts they put forth every day, the sacrifices they make, and the difference it makes brings back that hope and expectation that this "dream job" might be a place where they can make a difference. Actions speak louder than words—*acknowledge the obvious.*

Reciprocate

One easy way to see what people want in the form of appreciation is to look for what they give. For example, I take pride in being the sort of person who will try to accommodate almost any request. I will move things around in my schedule or sacrifice my own plans to help someone out if asked. I know I can always find a way to help out. In return, I hope for the same. I get frustrated when I ask for help and someone just immediately says, "I can't." I'm learning to recognize that we are all different and respond to requests for help differently, but I am so pleased when others are willing to help me out with the same generosity as I give. Do you know people who might feel the same?

My mother was the same way (it's true; this apple doesn't fall far from the tree). When she was working late and taking on so much at the office, she just hoped to see others who would be willing to sacrifice what they were doing to work out a way to provide some support. I don't want to misrepresent her experience at that office. She enjoyed her work and sincerely appreciated the job. She showed this by working hard and always being available. Another facet of her as an individual is that she also *loves* to cook. This is how she expresses love, commitment, and, yes, even appreciation. She is famous for her homemade cheesecake. One thing the office did right was making sure to celebrate her birthday in a way that she enjoyed, by sharing a potluck lunch of homemade dishes brought in by the staff. On those potluck days, she truly enjoyed being with the people in the company and always left the office smiling.

A dear friend of mine is wired completely differently. Her gift is being able to say the kindest things about people. She does this often to express her appreciation to me. She will go on for two or three minutes letting me know how much I provide when I listen to her or when I give her advice that she needs to hear. She uses words like *amazing, incredible,* and *immense.* Part of me wants to just roll my eyes because it sounds so flowery, and another part of me wants to curl up in a corner because I am just not that comfortable hearing someone say such nice things about me for so long!

But that's what she values. That's how she sees appreciation communicated.

So at least once a year, usually on her birthday, I prepare and deliver a two- or three-minute toast to the *amazing* gifts she brings to the people in her life and the *incredible* perspective she brings to me and the challenges I face, and the *immense* difference it makes for so many people in the world. She tears up every time.

So one way of identifying how people prefer to be appreciated is to see how they appreciate others and then reciprocate. Actions speak louder than words—*give them what they value!*

But What about the Poor Performers?

How do you appreciate someone who is simply not making the cut? As I said earlier, if the appreciation is generic or the same for everybody, you might undermine all of the other great things you do. But don't miss out on the fact that, while active appreciation is critical in building and sustaining good performance, it could also be the key to improving poor performance.

As mentioned earlier, bragging on someone calls that person to be more. Active appreciation of what poor performers are doing right allows them to feel some success. Despite all of the research, studies, and surveys done to confirm the value of positive reinforcement over focusing on the negative, the managers I work with struggle to find positive words to say, especially to poor performers. When coaching managers dealing with problem employees, the first task I give them is to *catch poor performers doing something right.*

One of the fundamental steps in driving change is to celebrate small victories.[2] When poor performers are doing some things well but struggling with others, active appreciation of their small successes can get them over the hump to improve in the other areas.

But beware...you must be genuine. It is not useful to puff up someone who is not doing a good job. This will only result in continued poor performance. All you need to do is catch those poor performers doing something right, and then acknowledge them for it, creating active appreciation.

If these sorts of active appreciation seem awkward or uncomfortable in the context of how your company currently communicates, that

[2] See http://blogs.hbr.org/2011/05/small-wins-and-feeling-good/

indicates that there is not currently a culture of active appreciation. Creating a culture does not just happen because it's a good idea and people want to start being that way. It takes time and commitment to specific actions.

Five

Creating a Contagious Culture of Active Appreciation

Creating a Contagious Culture of Active Appreciation

Culture can be defined as *how we do things.* To attempt any change or improvement without ensuring a culture that supports it is an exercise in futility. Most of your culture is defined and shaped by the conversations you have. In order to build a culture that fosters active appreciation, you must intentionally have conversations that do so. All of the acts of appreciation discussed in the previous chapter center around the conversations you have with your employees. Effective communication is a key driver to building a culture.

Individual personality plays a big role in how people perceive appreciation. There are many personality profiles that provide insight into these preferences. For example, Gary Chapman and Paul White have created a Motivating by Appreciation (MBA) Assessment (see *The 5 Languages of Appreciation in the Workplace* by Chapman and White) that identifies people's preference for feeling appreciated. However, if a personality profile or assessment is not available, there is only one sure way to know how people wish to be acknowledged: you have to ask them.

I have worked with organizations that specifically ask at the end of each assignment or project, "What would you like to be acknowledged for?" As a leader who would ask this of my team, I was often surprised with their responses. There were things I had taken for granted that they just needed to hear me acknowledge. For example, one of our employees lived more than thirty-five miles away and commuted to work early every day so that she could leave in time to miss the rush-hour traffic. Not doing so meant she lost an additional hour with her kids at night. To my astonishment, one afternoon after a team meeting that went on until 4:30 p.m., I asked her if there was anything about the meeting she would like to be acknowledged for. She said, "I'm gonna be stuck in traffic." It was a small thing. My first thought was, "Well, that's the price you pay for living so far away." But then I did what she asked.

I used active appreciation by thanking her for staying later and telling her I understood that doing so meant that she would not have as much time with her family that night. And then I told her that her being at the meeting provided answers to several important questions and a good foundation for the solutions we had all created. Her response was, "I was happy to help and will be sure to schedule to stay late for the next one."

Remember, the definition of appreciation includes *understanding*. The only way to truly understand what she valued and what she needed to hear so that she could feel understood and appreciated for her contribution was to ask her. In lieu of that, all I had were thoughts of what I would like to be appreciated for if I were her, and my views were nowhere close to what she needed to hear.

A note of caution: The only thing worse than not asking what people need is asking them and then ignoring their response. Ask, and then listen. And then acknowledge!

One more important point: While supervisors and leaders play a critical role in employees' feelings of appreciation, there is also a need to feel appreciated by coworkers and cross-functional peers. The quickest way to encourage employees to take on effective active appreciation is to allow them to see it in action by their leaders.

Peter Fuda wrote an article for the *Harvard Business Review* titled "Fire, Snowball, Mask, Movie: How Leaders Spark and Sustain Change."[3] His Snowball story involved a leader who was "exhausted by the passive culture in his company." After a startling 360 feedback review, the leader saw his leadership style and that of the company's management team as the cornerstone of how employees interacted with the company. He called upon his top leaders and committed to them that he would change his directive leadership style to one that called for interaction and feedback from them and all employees. He acknowledged that he had thought he was doing his best by using the directive style of leadership, but he wanted to heed the feedback he'd received and work toward a more effective leadership style, and he asked for his management team's support in his change. His leaders held him accountable for changing his leadership style. And then an amazing thing happened. The members of the management team also changed their leadership styles to one of engagement

---

[3] Peter Fuda, "Fire, Snowball, Mask, Movie: How Leaders Spark and Sustain Change," *Harvard Business Review* (November 2011).

and feedback. The result was that their company experienced a dramatic overhaul.

The fact that the leader led his company out of a bad place and into a good one certainly makes this a good story. To me, the most exciting element of the company's transformation was not the leader's shift, but the way the leader's shift changed everyone who worked with him. His commitment, conversations, and leadership styles were *contagious.* Once he gave up his directive approach and began truly developing a team, his leadership team did the same.

This is possible for the people in your company. Once leaders take on active appreciation, and do so in a way that effectively improves how people work for them and interact with them, others will follow suit. Success is contagious!

The fundamental element of a culture is its conversations. Set the example as a leader who builds active appreciation into your conversations, and you will see the culture of your team and throughout your organization move toward one where employees are engaged and contributing.

Conclusion

I've noticed that most people who love the idea of this book are people who do not feel appreciated. I have not had one single client ask me to write more about how they can express their appreciation better. Most managers assume that because they feel appreciative, their employees feel appreciated.

No matter if you are the CEO, COO, vice president, manager, or coworker, if you are looking for a more personal commitment from your team, you have to get personal with them. I'm not suggesting you question the entire hierarchical relationship you have with your team. What I *am* asking is that you take a look at how you appreciate the *persons* you work with. How do you give them what they need to succeed? How do you generate that feeling of *personal* pride in what they bring to the team and how they do their jobs?

I have yet to meet a manager who doesn't care about the people he or she works with. The critical piece in turning that care into a mutual, committed relationship is the personal communication required for active appreciation.

To those of you who have to venture into new and uncomfortable territory to have these conversations and follow through on these actions, thank you for your courage to be vulnerable and responsive to the needs of the people on your team. This book is not intended to be the final word on active appreciation, but the start of a journey, a *conversation*.

To those of you who have had to give up the idea that you have done all you can and the rest is up to the employees, thank you for being willing to give more for the sake of your team's success.

To those of you who have failed at fostering appreciation among your team despite your true heartfelt understanding of their value, thank you for being willing to change your approach.

Thank you for the leadership role you take on every day. Thank you for being willing to say, "This shall be done, because I say so." Thank you for being responsible and accountable for the success of your people, for your team, for your organization, and for the customers you serve.

You make a difference.

www.ingramcontent.com/pod-product-compliance
Lightning Source LLC
Chambersburg PA
CBHW051243170526
45165CB00004B/1552